THE LORDSHIP OF JESUS

THE LORDSHIP OF JESUS

A Study in Christian Discipleship

by
W. T. Purkiser

Beacon Hill Press of Kansas City
Kansas City, Missouri

ISBN: 083-411-1357

Printed in the
United States of America

Cover: Royce Ratcliff

KJV—King James Version.

Unless otherwise indicated, all scriptures are from the NIV.

10 9 8 7 6 5 4 3 2 1

Contents

Preface

This is a brief study of the meaning of the New Testament proclamation, "Jesus is Lord" (Rom. 10:9; 1 Cor. 12:3) and "Jesus Christ is Lord" (Phil. 2:11). It is an attempt to trace some of the very practical applications of the Lordship of Jesus.

That Jesus is Lord has both theological and practical meaning. In theological terms, it is a statement of His oneness in nature with the Father God and with the Holy Spirit. In practical terms, it points to the wonder of human redemption, to the will of God for our salvation. To exhaust the meaning of the Lordship of Jesus would be to sound the very depths of Christian truth.

It is with the practical meaning of the Lordship of Jesus that we are chiefly concerned here. To be a Christian at all is to be committed to life under the Lordship of Christ.

We look first at what it means that Jesus is Lord, then at what His Lordship means for us both in claim and privilege. That Jesus is Savior is affirmed 15 times in the New Testament; that Jesus is Lord is stated approximately 290 times.

The material presented here was prepared for the morning sessions of the Southern California District Holiness Crusade held on the campus of Point Loma Nazarene College, July 29 to August 4, 1985.

I am particularly indebted to Dr. Robert H. Scott, district superintendent; to administrative assistant Charles W. Ogden; and to Holiness Crusade Board Chairman R. Dean Shaw for a multitude of courtesies.

It is my sincere prayer that those who read these pages may know or come to know better Jesus Christ both as Savior and Lord.

1

JESUS IS LORD

These pages are born of the conviction that the Lordship of Jesus is basic to the whole of Christian faith and life. There is general agreement that the earliest Christian creed is expressed in the three words, "Jesus is Lord." Christians would and do believe much more. They can never believe less. That Jesus is Lord—when properly and biblically understood—is the key to all of Christian experience.

Such is the testimony of the New Testament. In Romans 10, the apostle Paul quotes a passage from Deuteronomy: "But what does it say? 'The word is near you; it is in your mouth and in your heart.'" He then applies it to the New Testament gospel: "That is, the word of faith we are proclaiming: That if you confess with your mouth, 'Jesus is Lord,' and believe in your heart that God raised him from the dead, you will be saved" (vv. 8-9).

The saving confession, "Jesus is Lord," is not just a matter of mouthing words. Paul states in 1 Cor. 12:3, "No one can say, 'Jesus is Lord,' except by the Holy Spirit." Central to the understanding of the Lordship of Jesus is the hymn quoted by the apostle in Philippians 2: "Your attitude should be the same as that of Christ Jesus:

Who, being in very nature God,
did not consider equality with God something
to be grasped,
but made himself nothing,
taking the very nature of a servant,

being made in human likeness.
And being found in appearance as a man,
he humbled himself
and became obedient to death—
even death on a cross!
Therefore God exalted him to the highest place
and gave him the name that is above every name,
that at the name of Jesus every knee should bow,
in heaven and on earth and under the earth,
and every tongue confess that Jesus Christ is Lord,
to the glory of God the Father *(vv. 5-11).*

What is the meaning of those simple but far-reaching words, *Kurios Iēsous,* "Jesus is Lord"? Few phrases are more common in current Christian speech; few are less understood.

Virtually everything we can say about Christ Jesus is implied in this affirmation of His Lordship: His deity, His humanity, His redemptive death, His resurrection life, His heavenly intercession, and His coming again in glory to reign—all that He was and is, taught and did, is involved in the simple affirmation, "Jesus is Lord."

The Name Above All

This is in part because of the unsuspected depth of meaning in the term "Lord." It is the "name that is above every name," given by the Father. The ultimate and final confession of all the sentient universe will be that "Jesus Christ is Lord, to the glory of God the Father" (Phil. 2:9, 11). The name "Lord" is above every name because it is God's own name.

There is therefore more in the name "Lord" than meets the eye. The term in the Hebrew Old Testament is *Adon/Adonai.* In New Testament Greek it is *Kurios.* Both the Hebrew and the Greek words may be used to describe human beings. They are used as terms of respect, comparable to our use of "Sir" and the Spanish use of "Señor." They are used of husbands and fathers in relation to members of the household. They are used of masters in relation to slaves. They are used of false gods, as when Paul speaks of "gods many, and lords many" (1 Cor. 8:5, KJV). In Roman times, the Greek *kurios* came to be used of the emperor.

But the most significant use of "lord" in both the Old and New Testaments is its use in reference to God. *Kurios* is used approximately 80 times in the New Testament with respect to human beings. It is used approximately 150 times to refer to the Father God. It is used at least 290 times in reference to the Lord Jesus.

The Meaning of "Lord"

In all its uses, three facts stand out in connection with the term itself:

(1) "Lord" is a relational term. It refers to a relationship between persons. Ownership in the barest sense may apply to things. One may own material objects or animals. But lordship has to do with a relationship between those who address each other as "You" and "I." It implies also a permanent relationship, not one that is temporary or transient.

(2) Lordship speaks of power that is absolute. It is total authority. The best illustration is that of the familiar biblical picture of master and slave. Slavery was a bitter fact of life in biblical times, and one aspect of it is picked up to illustrate the relationship between God and those who serve Him. Slaves lived under the absolute dominion of their masters. They belonged totally to those who owned them. The authority of the master was without limits.

(3) But lordship in its truest meaning also implies rightful authority—lawfulness. The exercise of power among men may be despotic—imposed without pretense of legality. But one who is truly lord is lord by reason of right as well as might.

In the divine Lordship, power and right are blended and essentially one. Werner Foerster claims that a realization of the highest meaning of lordship arises when man is confronted by the God who has created him in absolute power and is the absolute Authority "before which it is freedom rather than bondage to bow. . . . The ministering and forgiving love of God woos [man's] obedience and reconstructs all the relations of lordship."[1]

Lordship, then, is the relationship of power and rightful or valid authority between persons. The lord is one who has full authority, whose will is decisive, and to whom submission is due. To lose either the power or the right is fatal to the true nature of lordship. A human lord without power would be futile; without some sort of legitimacy he would be a despot. A God without power would be but a sort of "honorary president of the universe" who really doesn't matter. On the other hand, a God without right would be the kind of pagan deity who evokes superstition and fear, to whom loving service is impossible.

The Lord Is God

It is the use of "lord" in relation to God that concerns us here. The New Testament use has its roots in the Old Testament.

The first term for Deity in the Old Testament is *Elohim,* almost always translated "God." It is used some 2,200 times in all. It points to the creative power of the Almighty. It is the term consistently used in Gen. 1:1—2:3. It is also used occasionally for the "gods" worshiped in the pagan world. It is derived from the basic Semitic root for "God," whoever and whatever that god might be.

In Gen. 2:4, we meet the second and most meaningful name for the true and living God. It is *Yahweh.* Although known and used in worship from the time of Enosh, the son of Seth (Gen. 4:26), it was explained to Moses in Exod. 3:13-14 and 6:2-3 as the true God's own personal name. *Yahweh* is used some 6,800 times in the Old Testament, always in reference to the Lord God of Abraham, Isaac, and Jacob who revealed himself in Scripture. False gods could be called *Adon* and *El.* None but the true and living God was called *Yahweh.*

Yahweh is actually derived from the verb "to be" and is defined for Moses as meaning "I am who I am"—the eternally existent One who is present with His people. It is the covenant name of the true God whose worship became the distinctive mark of the people of Israel.

A third term used of God in the Old Testament is the term for "lord," *Adonai* (the plural of *Adon,* indicating dignity or worth). It was first used of God by Abraham in Gen. 15:2, 8 in connection with *Yahweh,* and thereafter about 340 times throughout the Old Testament.

The Sacred Name

Of crucial importance to the New Testament use of the term "Lord" is an intriguing bit of Jewish history. *Yahweh*—God's unique personal name—came to be regarded as so sacred and holy that it was never spoken aloud. When scribes copying the Old Testament Hebrew scriptures came to the name, they always used a new pen to write it. When rabbis reading the Scripture in Hebrew came to *Yahweh,* they always substituted *Adonai,* the Hebrew term meaning Lord.

Sometime shortly after about 200 B.C., because the Israelites were no longer speaking Hebrew but Aramaic or Greek, the famous Septuagint translation was made. The Hebrew scriptures were translated into Greek, and the Greek translation became the Bible of New Testament times. The majority of the quotations from the Old Testament made by New Testament writers are not from the Hebrew original but from the Septuagint Greek translation.

What would the translators do with the sacred name? Their choice was most significant. Following the long-established custom of using the Hebrew term for Lord instead of *Yahweh,* the translators chose the Greek equivalent *Kurios.* Most of the

English translations follow their lead. The KJV, RSV, NASB, NIV, and most English translations use LORD for *Yahweh.* To set it off from the occasional use of *Adonai* (Lord), the English versions print LORD with an initial capital and the remaining three letters in small capitals when the original Hebrew text reads *Yahweh.*[2]

The Name of Deity

What all this means is that when God gave Jesus the name above every name, He gave Him His own name—the name Lord. This is one of the clearest and most persuasive witnesses to the total and complete deity of the Savior. It becomes crystal clear when we consider the times the New Testament applies to Jesus statements from the Old Testament that refer to *Yahweh* (the LORD).

For example, Isa. 40:3 says, "A voice of one calling: 'In the desert prepare the way for the LORD *[Yahweh];* make straight in the wilderness a highway for our God.'" In the New Testament, these words are spoken of John the Baptist as he prepared the way for the public ministry of Jesus (Matt. 3:3; Mark 1:3; Luke 3:4; John 1:23).

Jer. 9:24 says, "Let him who boasts boast . . . [in] the LORD *[Yahweh]."* In 1 Cor. 1:31 and 2 Cor. 10:17, Paul applies these words to the Lord Jesus. Joel 2:32 promises, "Everyone who calls on the name of the LORD *[Yahweh]* will be saved." In Acts 2:21 by Peter and Rom. 10:13 by Paul, this promise is referred to Christ as the Lord upon whom we call for salvation.[3]

Indeed, as we previously noted, Jesus is called "Lord" throughout the New Testament 290 times, by that title alone or in combination with other titles or names. The list is impressive: the Lord; our Lord; the Lord Jesus Christ; Jesus Christ our Lord; Christ Jesus our Lord, or Christ Jesus my Lord or the Lord; Jesus our Lord; our Lord Christ; our Lord Jesus; the Lord Christ; and the Lord, Jesus Christ.

When we reflect that "LORD" stands for the great "I AM" who was the true God of the Old Testament (Exod. 3:14), the magnificent "I ams" of Jesus in the Gospel of John take on new meaning. "Before Abraham was born, I am!" Jesus said (8:58). The repetition is impressive:

"I am the bread of life" or "living bread" (6:35, 48, 51).
"I am the light of the world" (8:12).
"I am the gate for the sheep" (10:7, 9).
"I am the good shepherd" (10:11, 14).
"I am the resurrection and the life" (11:25).
"I am the way and the truth and the life" (14:6).
"I am the true vine" (15:1).

Proved by His Resurrection

That Jesus was Lord in nature, in what He is, from the moment of His conception, is indeed clear. But that Lordship was publicly demonstrated, open to all, at His resurrection and ascension. Because He had been obedient unto death, God gave Him the name Lord (Phil. 2:8-11). Peter proclaimed to his countrymen, "God has made this Jesus, whom you crucified, both Lord and Christ" (Acts 2:36).

It was the risen Christ who said to His disciples, "All authority in heaven and on earth has been given to me" (Matt. 28:18). And Paul told the Romans that "through the Spirit of holiness" Christ "was declared with power to be the Son of God by his resurrection from the dead: Jesus Christ our Lord" (1:4); and "For this very reason, Christ died and returned to life so that he might be the Lord of both the dead and the living" (14:9).

In Prayer and Worship

Jesus is addressed as Lord in worship and prayer. Paul wrote to "the church of God in Corinth, to those sanctified in Christ Jesus and called to be holy, together with all those everywhere who call on the name of our Lord Jesus Christ—their Lord and ours" (1 Cor. 1:2-3). To be a Christian is to call on or pray in the name of Jesus as Lord.

The dying martyr Stephen prayed, "Lord Jesus, receive my spirit" and "Lord, do not hold this sin against them" (Acts 7:59-60).

When the risen Redeemer appeared to Saul of Tarsus, Saul's response was the question, "Who are you, Lord?" (Acts 9:5; 22:8; 26:15). Admittedly, there may be less in the term "Lord" here than Paul came later to see. But the sense of the Divine Presence was undeniable.

When told that the heavenly Visitant was Jesus of Nazareth, whom he was persecuting, Paul immediately capitulated. "What shall I do, Lord?" was his submission to the authority of Jesus the Lord (Acts 22:9-10).

Paul himself led the way among New Testament writers in repeated affirmation of the Lordship of Jesus in all that it means. Afflicted with a thorn in the flesh, he records, "Three times I pleaded with the Lord to take it away."

When the answer came, it was not what Paul had expected, but it satisfied him completely. Jesus said, "My grace is sufficient for you, for my power is made perfect in weakness."

"Therefore," said the apostle, "I will boast all the more gladly about my weaknesses, so that Christ's power may rest on me. That is why, for Christ's sake, I delight in weaknesses, in insults, in hardships, in persecutions, in difficulties. For when I am weak, then I am strong" (2 Cor. 12:8-10). It was to Christ the Lord that Paul addressed his prayer, and from Christ the Lord he received the answer.

Paul links "our God and Father" with "our Lord Jesus" in prayer that the way may be cleared for him to go to Thessalonica. He adds, "May the Lord make your love increase and overflow for each other and for everyone else, just as ours does for you. May he strengthen your hearts so that you will be blameless and holy in the presence of our God and Father when our Lord Jesus comes with all his holy ones" (1 Thess. 3:11-13).

In the second Thessalonian letter, the apostle again prays, "May our Lord Jesus Christ himself and God our Father, who loved us and by his grace gave us eternal encouragement and good hope, encourage your hearts and strengthen you in every good deed and word" (2:16-17). He closes the letter with a benediction addressed to "the Lord of peace himself" that He may "give you peace at all times and in every way. The Lord be with all of you" (3:16).

But it was given to Thomas "the Doubter" to make the highest confession of all: "My Lord and my God!" This was an affirmation Jesus accepted without protest or question (John 20:28-29).

When we add it all together, there is little doubt that in receiving the name that is above every name, the name "Lord," Jesus is revealed for all time and to all people as One with the Father in the sublime mystery of the God who is Three in One.

The Scope of Christ's Lordship

To exhaust the New Testament treatment of the Lordship of Jesus would take volumes. A quick summary in five statements must suffice here:

1. *Jesus is Lord of creation.* Gen. 1:1 affirms, "In the beginning God created the heavens and the earth." The New Testament adds that God's Agent in creation was the Son, the divine Second Person of the Godhead, incarnate as Jesus Christ.

Thus the prologue to John's Gospel parallels the opening verse of Genesis with the statement: "In the beginning was the Word, and the Word was with God, and the Word was God. He was with God in the beginning. Through him all things were made; without him nothing was made that has been made. . . . He was in the world, and though the world was made through him, the world did not recognize him" (1:1-3, 10).

Paul makes the same point in Col. 1:15-16: "He is the image of the invisible God, the firstborn over all creation. For by him all things were created: things in heaven and on earth, visible and invisible, whether thrones or powers or rulers or authorities; all things were created by him and for him."

The writer to the Hebrews begins his masterful comparison of the Christian gospel with the older revelation with the words, "In the past God spoke to our forefathers through the prophets at many times and in various ways, but in these last days he has spoken to us by his Son, whom he appointed heir of all things, and through whom he made the universe" (Heb. 1:1-2).

The legitimacy of Christ's Lordship starts here. We are rightfully His because He made us. In a much misunderstood passage in Romans 9, Paul asks the rhetorical question, "But who are you, O man, to talk back to God? 'Shall what is formed say to him who formed it, "Why did you make me like this?" [a quotation from Isa. 29:16; 45:9].' Does not the potter have the right to make out of the same lump of clay some pottery for noble purposes and some for common use?" (vv. 20-21). God has indeed made us in His own image as creatures with capacity to respond to His offered grace and therefore to choose whether we shall be "for noble purposes" or "for common use." He wills to have mercy on all who call on His name in obedient faith (10:8-13; 11:32). But the point of the question stands. Christ the Lord as Creator does have authority over what and those He has made.

2. *Jesus is Lord of history.* It was His birth that divided the centuries into "Before" and "After" (A.D., *anno Domini,* "in the year of our Lord"). His coming into the world constituted the fullness of time (Gal. 4:4).

Men base their philosophies of history on dominant human personalities, economic forces, geography, or other influences and explanations. But for the Christian, history is, as is so often said, "His story." His is a kingdom of grace that has come. It is a kingdom of glory that is coming.

3. *Jesus is Lord of the present.* Charles Haddon Spurgeon, the great London pastor-evangelist, related that he once battled severe discouragement in his ministry. He sat brooding one day in his study when his eye was caught by a biblical motto on his desk. It was a quotation from Heb. 13:8, "Jesus Christ the same yesterday, and to day, and for ever" (KJV). The words that leaped out at him were the words "to day." Yesterday and forever are important; but we live in the present. If Christ were not Lord today, He would not be Lord at all.

4. *Jesus is Lord of the future.* He is the "Alpha" (the first letter of the Greek alphabet), "the Beginning." He is also the "Omega" (the last letter), "the End" (Rev. 22:13).[4] His coming again is the consummation toward which all history moves. When He will come is known to the Father alone (Matt. 24:36; Mark 13:32; Acts 1:8). *That* He will come shortly is the confidence and hope of all who love His appearing (James 5:8; 2 Pet. 3:10-12; Rev. 22:12, 20).

5. *Jesus is Lord of ALL.* He is King of Kings and Lord of Lords. That God is indeed King of Kings and Lord of Lords is the faith of the Old Testament (Deut. 10:17; Ps. 136:3). That the Father has given to the Son to be King of Kings and Lord of Lords is the message of the New Testament (1 Tim. 6:15; Rev. 17:14; 19:16).

It is this that makes the paradox of the Servant-Lord so poignant. Jesus told His disciples, "You know that those who are regarded as rulers of the Gentiles lord it over them, and their high officials exercise authority over them. Not so with you. Instead, whoever wants to become great among you must be your servant, and whoever wants to be first must be slave of all. For even the Son of Man did not come to be served, but to serve, and to give his life as a ransom for many"

(Mark 10:42-45). "I am among you as one who serves," He said (Luke 22:27).

In fact, the very point of the great Kenosis (Greek term for "emptying") passage in Phil. 2:5-11 is that we should have the attitude of the Servant-Lord in ourselves in humble obedience and service in the Body of Christ. In this, our Example is none other than the Lord of all.

No distant Lord have I,
Loving afar to be.
Made flesh for me He cannot rest
Until He rests in me.

I need not journey far
This dearest Friend to see.
Companionship is always mine;
He makes His home with me.

I envy not the Twelve.
Nearer to me is He.
The life He once lived here on earth
He lives again in me.

Ascended now to God
My witness there to be,
His witness here am I because
His Spirit dwells in me.

O glorious Son of God,
Incarnate Deity,
I shall forever be with Thee
Because Thou art with me.

—MALTBIE D. BABCOCK

2

RECONCILIATION: ACCEPTANCE OF THE LORDSHIP OF JESUS

That Jesus is Lord is eternally true whether anyone accepts it now or not. But the Lordship of Jesus becomes real for us individually in that gracious act of redemption the Bible knows as reconciliation. Here again the words of Paul in Rom. 10:9-10 become central: "If you confess with your mouth, 'Jesus is Lord,' and believe in your heart that God raised him from the dead, you will be saved. For it is with your heart that you believe and are justified, and it is with your mouth that you confess and are saved." And in verse 13, Paul quotes the words of Joel 2:32, "Everyone who calls on the name of the Lord will be saved." There is a total vision of redemption in the simple words, *Kurios Iēsous,* "Jesus is Lord."

The Incarnation

Jesus, we recall, is the human name of the Savior. It is the English rendering of the Greek form of Joshua, the Old Testament name that means "The Lord is salvation," or "The Lord saves."

There were others in New Testament times named Joshua or Jesus. Two of them appear in the New Testament: the disciple whose name was "Jesus, who is called Justus" (Col. 4:11), and the father of Elymas the sorcerer in Acts 13:6, 8 (Bar-Jesus means “son of Jesus”). This is why in the Gospels, Jesus is often identified as “Jesus of Nazareth” or “Jesus who is called Christ.”

“Jesus” stands for the fact of the Incarnation. Incarnation simply means that the eternal Son of God became a human being. We remember again the stately words of John, “In the beginning was the Word, and the Word was with God, and the Word was God. . . . The Word became flesh and made his dwelling among us” (1:1, 14). The Redeemer is not unreachable, unapproachable Deity, but “the man Christ Jesus” (1 Tim. 2:5).

Jesus is our Mediator by reason of the fact of His unique nature as the God-man. He can reach up and touch God. But He can also reach down and grasp our hands and bring us to God in reconciliation. He became the Son of Man that we through Him might become the children of God. In Charles Wesley’s memorable hymn-lines:

Jesus! the name that charms our fears,
That bids our sorrows cease;
’Tis music in the sinner’s ears;
’Tis life, and health, and peace.

He breaks the pow’r of canceled sin;
He sets the pris’ner free.
His blood can make the foulest clean;
His blood availed for me.

Our Need of Reconciliation

Our need of reconciliation lies in the most basic fact about our unredeemed humanity. We are creatures estranged from our Creator, living in rebellion, wandering in the far country of self-will—the exaggerated self-sovereignty that is the essence of sin. By the gross misuse of our God-given freedom, we have sold ourselves into slavery. We are aliens by birth; we are rebels by choice.

There is an admitted paradox here. The sovereignty of the Lord God is real and absolute. His will is supreme. Yet one meaning of the divine image in our humanity is that the Sovereign God has endowed us with a measure of freedom such that we can even say no to Him. In fact, as Scottish theologian John Macquarrie has argued, this division of sovereign power is really the highest manifestation of God's absolute sovereignty.[1] A God less than totally sovereign would not dare give His creatures such a choice.

Georgia Harkness puts it this way:

> That God is the sovereign Lord of human destinies and that man is in some sense a free spirit are foundation stones of Christian faith. These two affirmations do not comprise the whole of Christian theology, but they make all the rest of it an organic structure. Remove either of these foundations, and the structure either collapses or requires extraneous props for its support.[2]

And A. W. Tozer comments:

> God sovereignly decreed that man should be free to exercise moral choice, and man from the beginning has fulfilled the decree by making his choice between good and evil. When he chooses to do evil, he does not thereby countervail the sovereign will of God but fulfills it, inasmuch as the eternal decree decided not which choice the man should make but that he would be free to make it. . . . Man's will is free because God is sovereign. A God less than sovereign could not bestow moral freedom upon His creatures. He would be afraid to do so.[3]

This balance of divine sovereignty and human freedom is what gives meaning and relevance to the concept of the kingdom of God or the kingdom of Christ as it is developed throughout the Bible. Some theologians place a one-sided emphasis on the sovereignty of God to the degree that they affirm individual human destiny to be decided from all eternity by the divine decree and any genuine human freedom to be unreal.

These thinkers have failed to understand the meaning of the use of "kingdom" as an illustration of the relationship between God and man. With the exception of the years Israel lived as a theocracy, biblical man lived under the total sovereignty known in ancient empires and kingdoms. The will of the king was absolute; he had complete power of life and death over all his citizens. Yet the total sovereignty of the monarch did not mean that individual citizens were controlled like puppets on strings or robots working out an inner programming. Ancient kings and emperors knew well the possibility of citizens in rebellion, in disobedience, and ultimately under judgment. Such was the relationship of David and Absalom and his followers and Solomon with Jeroboam when Israel split apart. The greatest sovereign was not one who could control each choice of his subjects but who could win their love and loyalty by his fairness and justice.

The Kingdom of God

The New Testament picks up on the concept of the Kingdom. Jesus had much to say about it. The Lord places His teaching about the Kingdom in a threefold time frame: (1) The Kingdom is at hand. Christ's first preaching was, "The time is fulfilled, and the kingdom of God is at hand. Repent, and believe in the gospel" (Mark 1:15, NKJV). (2) The Kingdom has arrived. Jesus said, "The kingdom of God does not come with your careful observation, nor will people say, 'Here it is,' or 'There it is,' because the kingdom of God is within you" (Luke 17:20-21). (3) The Kingdom is yet to come. We are to pray for the coming of the Kingdom: "This . . . is how you should pray: . . . your kingdom come, your will be done on earth as it is in heaven" (Matt. 6:9-10).

Any sense of contradiction dissolves when we reflect on the meaning of the term "kingdom." It is quite basically "the King's domain," where the King rules, where His will is accepted as the norm for life and being. The Kingdom was known in the good news of the arrival of the saving Lord (the gospel). The Kingdom is in our hearts through His Spirit. The Kingdom will be over all the earth when "Jesus shall reign where'er the sun / does his successive journeys run."

Alan Richardson reminds us that the phrase "kingdom of God" in the English versions of the New Testament may not be the best translation of the Greek phrase *hē basileia tou Theou. Basileia* strictly means "reign" or "sovereignty"—"kingship" rather than "kingdom." "It is," Richardson says, "not so much a place over which God rules as God's reign itself."

Richardson goes on to say that the Kingdom came with power at Pentecost as Jesus predicted it would (Matt. 16:28; Mark 9:1; Luke 9:27). He adds that to enter the Kingdom means more than to become a subject; it means to "receive a share in God's Kingship," to be one of those appointed to reign. It was God's good pleasure to give "the reign" to His little flock (Luke 12:32).[4]

As Godfrey F. Bradby wrote:

The kingdoms of the Earth go by
In purple and in gold;
They rise, they triumph, and they die,
And all their tale is told.
One Kingdom only is divine,
One banner triumphs still;
Its King a servant, and its sign
A cross upon a hill.

Our Response to Jesus as Savior: Repentance

Jesus makes it clear what our response to the King must be: "The kingdom of God is at hand: repent . . . , and believe the gospel" (Mark 1:15, KJV). One can only wonder if repentance has not become the missing note in modern evangelicalism.

Perhaps part of the difficulty is that repentance is thought to be an emotion, an upheaval of feeling. Repentance may and should involve our feelings—but it must go much deeper. Repentance is more than emotion; it is decision.

The New Testament word for repentance is *metanoia.* It literally means a change of mind, of outlook, of viewpoint. John Wesley identified it with what he called "preventing grace" or "convincing grace."[5]

Repentance is in its original meaning a "turning around," turning one's back on sin and the old life and turning toward Christ. Dwight L. Moody gave an unforgettable definition of repentance when he recalled the testimony of an old soldier who said, "I was marching down the high road to perdition when the Captain of my salvation called, 'Halt! Right-about-face! Forward march!'"

Nothing less than this is our proper human response to the Lordship of Jesus. In the classic historical novel of New Testament times, *Quo Vadis?* there is the story of a young Roman centurion named Marcus Vinicius who fell in love with Lygia Callina, a Christian girl. Because he was a pagan, she refused to return his affection. Unknown to her one night, Marcus followed her to a secret meeting of the Christians. There he stood outside and listened to the apostle Peter preach.

As Marcus listened, something happened inside him. He came to see that Jesus Christ is the most important reality in life. But, as the author describes it, he "felt that, if he wished to follow that teaching, he would have to place on a burning pile all his thoughts, habits, and character, his whole nature up to that moment, burn them into ashes, and then fill himself with a life altogether different, and an entirely new soul."[6]

Saving Faith

What the author says about the life altogether different and the entirely new soul points to an authentic element in regard to repentance: It always involves a turning to Christ in faith.

Without such faith, repentance is little different from remorse or human reformation.

As the two very different convex and concave sides of a lens, so repentance and faith are two sides to one and the same act. As one cannot turn his back toward the north without turning his face to the south, so one cannot turn his back on sin without turning to Christ in faith. And, be it said, one cannot turn to Christ in saving faith who is not willing to turn his back on everything he knows to be sinful in the old life.

Again, there is a popular misunderstanding here. Saving faith is not mere assent of the mind to the truth of the gospel. Saving faith is wholehearted commitment to Christ in sincere reliance on His forgiveness and His gift of transforming grace.

It is easy to confuse opinions with faith. Opinions are what we argue about; faith is what we live by. There is no New Testament faith without obedience to Christ's Word. Paul, in Rom. 1:5, talks about "the obedience that comes from faith," or, as A. M. Hunter has somewhere said, "the obedience which faith is." It makes no difference whether we talk about believing the gospel (Mark 1:15, KJV) or obeying the gospel (Rom. 10:16, KJV; 2 Thess. 1:8; 1 Pet. 4:17). They amount to the same thing.

Just as We Are

Such faith is the sole condition for acceptance with Christ, for reconciliation with God and the power of a new life. We must always recognize that *God loves us enough to accept us just as we are.* None is too bad, too self-righteous, too stained and defeated—if he will but come.

The story of Charlotte Elliott is well known. This high-spirited, well-bred young English society girl became deeply concerned about her soul as the result of a conversation with a minister friend of the family. She asked him how she could find the Savior.

"I don't know how to come to Him," she said.

His reply was, "Come just as you are." Charlotte immortalized these words in her oft-sung hymn:

Just as I am, without one plea
But that Thy blood was shed for me,
And that Thou bidd'st me come to Thee,
O Lamb of God, I come! I come!

Just as I am, and waiting not
To rid my soul of one dark blot,
To Thee whose blood can cleanse each spot,
O Lamb of God, I come! I come!

Just as I am, though tossed about
With many a conflict, many a doubt,
Fightings and fears within, without,
O Lamb of God, I come! I come!

Just as I am—Thou wilt receive,
Wilt welcome, pardon, cleanse, relieve;
Because Thy promise I believe,
O Lamb of God, I come! I come!

Just as I am! Thy love unknown
Hath broken ev'ry barrier down;
Now to be Thine, yea, Thine alone,
O Lamb of God, I come! I come!

Forgiveness

What happens when we are "accepted in the beloved" (Eph. 1:6, KJV) is what the theologians call justification; the record of a sinful past is blotted out. "He who conceals his sins does not prosper, but whoever confesses and renounces them finds mercy" (Prov. 28:13). "If we confess our sins, he is faithful and just and will forgive us our sins and purify us from all unrighteousness" (1 John 1:9).

Corrie ten Boom, the delightful Dutch saint who wrote *The Hiding Place* and *Tramp for the Lord,* described her conversion in the words: "When I confessed my sins, the Lord took them and buried them in the deepest sea and then put up a sign for the devil, 'No fishing allowed!'"

The wonder of forgiveness is that, while it does not change the past, it breaks its power over us. It changes the meaning of the past for us and delivers us from its bondage. We have already quoted Charles Wesley's lines: forgiveness "breaks the pow'r of canceled sin [and] sets the pris'ner free."

New Life

But when we talk about justification and forgiveness, we must always add something vitally important: God loves us enough to accept us as we are; but *He loves us too much to leave us as we are.* Along with justification is regeneration, a new creation, a new level and dimension of life.

We are, in traditional terms, "born again." "In his great mercy he has given us new birth into a living hope through the resurrection of Jesus Christ from the dead" (1 Pet. 1:3). Paul writes, "He has rescued us from the dominion of darkness and brought us into the kingdom of the Son he loves, in whom we have redemption, the forgiveness of sins" (Col. 1:13-14)—a Kingdom we enter only by being "born again," "born of . . . the Spirit" (John 3:3-7).

A friend asked George Whitefield, the great 18th-century evangelist, why he so often preached on the text, "Ye must be born again." His reply was simple: "Because ye must be born again."

This is a note we must never lose. Dietrich Bonhoeffer, the Lutheran minister martyred by Adolf Hitler in the closing days of World War II, wrote a book titled *The Cost of Discipleship.* The thesis of the book is that much of Christendom suffers from a profound misunderstanding of grace and justification. A reviewer comments, "We have perverted the doctrine of the justification of the *sinner* into the justification of the *sin.*" As a result, we have been flooded with "cheap grace": Christianity without consequences in life.[7]

There is no possible substitute for transforming grace—not only as an attitude in the mind of God (His unmerited favor) but as a power working within the soul. Someone remarked that education says, "Learn again"; philosophy says, "Think again"; sociology says, "Work again"; sectarianism says, "Join again"; creedalism says, "Believe again"; Jesus says, "Be born again."

The Cost of Reconciliation

This acceptance and reconciliation is provided for us at supreme cost. It is in the cross of the Lord that we find forgiveness and freedom from the claims and chains of sin. We cannot fully explain but we may faithfully proclaim the fact of reconciliation with God through the death and resurrection of the Savior-Lord.

Bible students have long noted two strands of explanation for the Atonement in the New Testament. One is that on the Cross, Jesus offered the perfect and only adequate sacrifice for sins and thereby made possible a just forgiveness for all mankind. He took it upon himself to provide an acceptable substitute for our transgressions (e.g., Rom. 3:21-26). The other is that on the Cross Jesus met and defeated the evil powers of sin and death and thereby liberated us for our true life as children of the God who created us for himself. The Lord Jesus is *Christus Victor,* the Champion who won victory for us by defeating our eternal enemy (e.g., Col. 2:13-15).

Each of these strands of explanation is vital. Together they answer to our two great needs in relation to God. We are sinners under a debt to divine law we cannot pay. But we are also captives under the power of evil from which we cannot release ourselves. Through Christ, God both forgives the sins of which we are guilty and frees us from the sin that binds us.

Tourists tell of a famous intersection in London known as

Charing Cross. It is common for people to make appointments: "Meet me at the Cross." John May tells of a little lad who lived not far from Charing Cross. One day he wandered off and became lost. An English bobby was trying to help him. The lad remembered his name but not his address. Finally, the boy said, "Sir, take me to the Cross. I can find my way home from there."

Adam Baum wrote the lines:

I know no human Savior—
No Christ that men invent!
I only know the Christ of God—
Him whom the Father sent!

No human Christ could save me,
Nor from my sins set free;
The only Christ I worship
Is the Christ of Calvary!

The Purpose of Reconciliation

The purpose of forgiveness and reconciliation through the living Lord is discipleship. Discipleship is bringing more and more of life under the Lordship of Jesus.

Jesus asked the searching question, "Why do you call me, 'Lord, Lord,' and do not do what I say?" (Luke 6:46). And Matthew quotes the Master: "Not everyone who says to me, 'Lord, Lord,' will enter the kingdom of heaven, but only he who does the will of my Father who is in heaven" (Matt. 7:21).

A medieval hymn, picked up and popularized in recent years, says it well:

Day by day, day by day,
O dear Lord, three things I pray:
To see Thee more clearly,
To love Thee more dearly,
To follow Thee more nearly,
Day by day!

David Hubbard writes:

> This Lord Jesus, to whom we bear witness, is no sentimental dropout, no Palestinian flower child, no mere carpenter doing nice things for abused people. He is utterly, totally, absolutely, finally, Lord. Our response to his lordship as declared in his new teaching is not just speculation or even admiration. It is obedience, pure and simple. But in that obedience is freedom, true and magnificent.[8]

Many have known and pondered Anna Olander's lines as translated into English:

If I gained the world, but not the Savior,
Were my life worth living for a day?
Could my yearning heart find rest and comfort
In the things that soon must pass away?
If I gained the world, but not the Savior,
Would my gain be worth the lifelong strife?
Are all earthly pleasures worth comparing
For a moment with a Christ-filled life?

If I gained the world, but not the Savior,
Who endured the Cross and died for me,
Could then all the world afford a refuge
Whither, in my anguish, I might flee?

Oh, what emptiness without the Savior
'Mid the sins and sorrows here below!
And eternity, how dark without Him!
Only night and tears and endless woe!

Peter is right: "Salvation is found in no one else, for there is no other name under heaven given to men by which we must be saved" (Acts 4:12).

Christina Rossetti caught this truth in her four hymn-lines:

None other Lamb, none other name,
None other hope in heaven or earth or sea,

None other hiding place from guilt and shame.
None beside Thee.

In his book *Approaching Hoofbeats,* Dr. Billy Graham quotes an anonymous poet:

You asked me how I gave my heart to Christ,
I do not know;
There came a yearning for Him in my soul
So long ago;
I found earth's flowers would fade and die,
I wept for something that would satisfy,
And then, and then, somehow I seemed to dare
To lift my broken heart to God in prayer.
I do not know, I cannot tell you how;
I only know He is my Savior now.[9]

3

CONSECRATION: ESTABLISHMENT OF THE LORDSHIP OF JESUS

If our human response to Jesus as Savior is penitent faith, our human response to Jesus as Lord is consecration. Implied in our reconciliation with God is the promise of obedience. What we generally know as consecration makes explicit and practical what repentance implies.

Robert J. Hastings put it this way: "From the very start of his public ministry, one fact stands out in the conditions Jesus laid down for discipleship: he never asked a man for less than his total life. He did not ask for a fragmentary discipleship."[1] And Thomas R. Kelly wrote, "Totalitarian are the claims of Christ. No vestige of reservation of 'our' rights can remain."[2]

The Gospels are full of the radical, unconditional demands of Christ on His disciples. No halfhearted easy believism or cheap grace will do. Jesus called His followers to enter the Kingdom open-eyed, counting the cost.

Typical of this are the parables cited in Luke 14, where a man planning to build a tower is said always to count the cost to see whether he can finish it, and a king going out to battle considers whether with 10,000 troops he can meet an enemy with 20,000. The meaning of the two parables is summarized in verse 33, "In the same way, any of you who does not give up everything he has cannot be my disciple."

The Call to Consecration

Writing to the Christians at Rome, Paul three times over stresses the need for Christian consecration: "Offer yourselves to God, as those who have been brought from death to life; and offer the parts of your body to him as instruments of righteousness" (6:13); "Just as you used to offer the parts of your body in slavery to impurity and to ever-increasing wickedness, so now offer them in slavery to righteousness leading to holiness" (v. 19); and, "Therefore, I urge you, brothers, in view of God's mercy, to offer your bodies as living sacrifices, holy and pleasing to God—this is your spiritual act of worship. Do not conform any longer to the pattern of this world, but be transformed by the renewing of your mind. Then you will be able to test and approve what God's will is—his good, pleasing and perfect will" (12:1-2). And Peter urges his readers, "In your hearts set apart Christ as Lord" (1 Pet. 3:15).

Theologically, the Lordship of Jesus testifies to His full and complete deity, His oneness in nature with God. Practically, the Lordship of Jesus calls us to the act of self-giving in consecration that establishes His reign in our personal lives.

Repentance and Consecration

We need to take a look at some of the essential differences between repentance as the gateway to Christian experience and consecration as the call to full discipleship.

1. In repentance, we come as those who have been living apart from God, heedless of His will, in virtual rebellion against His law, but now surrendering and yielding to Christ's authority. In consecration, we come as children of God by a new birth, yielding our lives and love to the full possession of Christ as Lord.

2. In repentance, we give up the sins and evils that have marred our lives in the past. In consecration, we yield a redeemed personality, a self made new, "acceptable unto God"

(Rom. 12:1, KJV), for His possession through all time. Every good talent, ability, and capacity is surrendered to Him.

Frances Ridley Havergal, the gifted Anglican author and poet whose "consecration hymn" we shall look at in a moment, wrote:

> He who made every power can use every power—memory, judgment, imagination, quickness of apprehension or insight; specialties of musical, poetical, oratorical, or artistic faculty; special tastes for reasoning, philosophy, history, natural science, or natural history—all of these may be dedicated to Him, sanctified by Him, and used by Him. Whatever He has given, He will use, if we will let Him.[3]

3. At the risk of some oversimplification, repentance may be said to be motivated usually by guilt, fear of the righteous judgment and wrath of God, or at least by the deep frustration of an unredeemed life. In consecration, most typically we are motivated by love, by a sincere desire to please the Savior. There may indeed be an element of imperative, a sense of duty, in consecration. But the dominant feeling is aspiration for the total will of God in our lives.

Many have seen an illustration of consecration in the provision for the "love slave" described in Exodus 21. An indentured Hebrew could be required to serve for no longer than six years. In the seventh year, he must be free to leave his master's household with whatever he had brought with him. However, what he had acquired during his years of service would remain in the household. "But if the servant declares, 'I love my master and my wife and children and do not want to go free,' then his master must take him before the judges. He shall take him to the door or the doorpost and pierce his ear with an awl. Then he will be his servant for life" (vv. 5-6).

D. Shelby Corlett remarks:

> It is evident that this emphasis upon consecration being a love-gift is contrary to any coercive act of giving, an act which

would have little love in it. Yet this stress is sometimes placed upon Christians as the basis of their consecration. Seemingly it is thought that the greater the struggle involved in giving oneself to God, the more real is the consecration. Occasionally a testimony of this nature is heard: "It nearly killed me to say 'yes' to God; but finally I yielded." That may be the attitude of a rebellious person making a surrender to God, but is it the worshipful act of making a present, a love-gift, of oneself to God in consecration?[4]

4. Repentance has to do chiefly with one's way of life. It is a reversal, a right-about-face. Consecration, on the other hand, has to do with the very essence of the self. It is more than the giving of time, talents, and treasure. The very citadel of self-life must be turned over to the Lord.

Mildred Dienert recalls that she had been shocked into repentance in part through an automobile accident in which several of her teenage companions were killed. She remembers that she had said in effect, "All right, Lord, here's my life." Yet, she said, there were reservations in her heart: it was "as though I said to God, 'You can have my life, but give me myself.'"[5] But it is that very self that must be yielded. God must have all of us before we can have all of His will.

We mentioned earlier Frances Ridley Havergal's description of the talents and abilities God can use. Better known is her consecration hymn, "Take My Life, and Let It Be." The poem opens with the lines, "Take my life, and let it be / Consecrated, Lord, to Thee." Then it becomes very specific:

Take my hands, and let them move
At the impulse of Thy love.

Take my feet, and let them be
Swift and beautiful for Thee.
Take my voice, and let me sing
Always, only, for my King.

Take my lips, and let them be
Filled with messages for Thee.
Take my silver and my gold;
Not a mite would I withhold.

Take my will and make it Thine;
It shall be no longer mine.
Take my heart, it is Thine own!
It shall be Thy royal throne.

Take my love; my God, I pour
At Thy feet its treasure store.

Each of these specifics—feet, voice, lips, silver and gold, will, heart, love—is a vitally important and essential part of consecration. If any one is unyielded, it becomes a source of defeat in the Christian life. But the true essence of consecration is in the last two lines:

Take myself and I will be
Ever, only, all for Thee.

5. Perhaps one final point should be made: Repentance has to do with the renunciation of what the writer to the Hebrews calls "dead works" (6:1, KJV) or "acts that lead to death" (NIV). It is coming out of death. Consecration, on the other hand, has to do with a "living sacrifice" made by one who is "alive from the dead" (Rom. 12:1; 6:13, both KJV). It is coming into the fullness of life.

Because unconverted persons are "dead in . . . transgressions and sins" (Eph. 2:1), they cannot offer a living sacrifice. In this sense, consecration is something only a born-again Christian can do.

This is clearly pictured in the Old Testament instructions concerning the sacrifices of the Jewish altar. The animal brought to the altar was to be a living animal. No dead carcass was ever offered as a sacrifice at the altar of God.

Furthermore, the sacrifice brought to God was to be

healthy and sound. Gerald Cragg comments on Rom. 12:1, "It is sacrilege complacently to bring to God lives whose stains have not been cleansed by repentance and renewal." He adds, "To be careless in God's service is more grievous sacrilege than it ever was to offer unclean beasts upon the altar." He also points out that the "holiness which is to be the mark of the life devoted to God is not expressed in esoteric ritual observances, but in the disciplines of ordinary experience."[6] In the midst of daily life we are to serve God "without fear in holiness and righteousness before him all our days" (Luke 1: 74-75).

Implied in all of this is the fact that consecration is not to some aspect of God's work with part of our capacities. It is to God himself and His full will with all there is of us. The Quaker commentator Dougan Clark reminds us that the command to yield ourselves to God included everything else. "All the details are included in the one surrender of yourself. . . . Consecration is the willingness, and the resolution, and the purpose to be, to do, and to suffer all God's will."[7]

Consecration and Sanctification

Well known is the fact that the verb "to sanctify" has a double meaning both in New Testament Greek and in English. It carries a primary Old Testament meaning: to set apart, to dedicate to God, to consecrate to sacred purposes. But it also means to make holy, to free from sin.

The first meaning of the term represents what we are called upon to do in response to the Lordship of Jesus. We are to yield, present, or consecrate ourselves. This is the meaning of the term in such familiar Old Testament passages as Exod. 13:2, where Moses is told by God, "Sanctify unto me all the firstborn, whatsoever openeth the womb among the children of Israel, both of man and of beast: it is mine" (KJV), or "Consecrate to me every firstborn male. The first offspring of every womb among the Israelites belongs to me, whether man or animal" (NIV); and Lev. 11:44, "For I am the LORD your God: ye shall therefore sanctify yourselves, and ye shall be holy; for I am holy" (KJV), or "I am the LORD your God; consecrate yourselves and be holy, because I am holy" (NIV).

But the second meaning is the one that becomes predominant in the New Testament. Here, to sanctify is not something we are to do for others or ourselves. Here, to sanctify is what God does for us in answer to consecration and faith. This is the second meaning of the term, to make holy or to free from sin.

There is one important passage in the New Testament where the two meanings come together. It is in the high-priestly prayer of Jesus, recorded in John 17. Here Jesus prays, "Sanctify them by the truth; your word is truth. As you sent me into the world, I have sent them into the world. For them I sanctify myself, that they too may be truly sanctified" (vv. 17-19).

When we ask in what sense Jesus would sanctify himself, it is evident that it could not mean to make himself holy or free from sin. He had been born the holy Son of God and never personally experienced sin either in heart or life.

What it does mean is that He would set himself apart, dedicate or consecrate himself to Calvary in order that His people might "be truly sanctified"—a verb in the perfect tense, indicating something accomplished with enduring results. It is the blood of His cross that "cleanses us from all sin" (1 John 1:7, NKJV), that truly sanctifies.

In this prayer, then, Jesus uses the clause, "I sanctify myself" in the clear sense of consecrating himself to death on the Cross. But as related to the disciples, to sanctify means something they are to have done for and in them in the deeper sense of being cleansed from inner sin and made holy. It is ours to consecrate ourselves as sacrifices on God's altar; it is

God's to seal those sacrifices with His cleansing and empowering Spirit.

The Time Factor

It is important to notice the time factor in consecration. Consecration is the act of a moment, something that occurs at a given time and place. But it is also the controlling attitude of all the rest of life.

These facts come out clearly in Paul's exhortations in Romans 6 and 12. Where Paul says in 6:13 and 19, "Offer yourselves to God" and "Offer [the parts of your body] in slavery to righteousness leading to holiness," the command to offer is in the timeless Greek aorist tense that indicates an act or process viewed as finished or complete.

But the purpose of the offering is to make Christ the continuing Lord of both person and life. The parts of our bodies —all our powers and capacities—are to be devoted to Him as "instruments of righteousness" (6:13) "in slavery to righteousness leading to holiness" (v. 19)—a continuous and ongoing state or condition.

In Rom. 12:1-2, similarly, Paul phrases the injunction "to offer your bodies as living sacrifices" in the aorist tense. It is something to do—decisively and now. But he speaks of being transformed and testing and approving God's will in the present tense: literally, "go on being transformed by the renewing of your mind," and "go on testing and approving what God's will is—his good, pleasing and perfect will."

Perhaps no better paradigm of the time factor in consecration and entire sanctification can be found than the familiar biblical analogy of the relationship between God and human persons as marriage. There is a distinction between a wedding and the marriage that follows. The wedding, like the act of consecration, takes place at a given point in time. It is a transaction that is soon completed. But the marriage goes on— despite the cynicism of the California jeweler who advertises wedding rings for rent—week after week, month after month, year after year, "till death us do part."

Nor does the bride ever know all that is involved in her promises "for better—for worse, for richer—for poorer, in sickness and in health." Consecration means putting on God's altar not only what we know but what used to be called "the unknown bundle"—for most of us, by far the larger part of the transaction.

When a man asks a maid to marry him, he does not give her a blueprint of the future with all its details. He may have plans for their life together, but both know that these plans may not work out. What he is asking is that she trust herself to him, that she make a personal commitment to himself on the basis of what she has come to know of his character. Such trust is the basis of the whole transaction. In the same way, we too give ourselves to our heavenly Bridegroom.

And, be it said, this is a lifetime process: forming the habit of "consciously involving Jesus Christ in every event of every day of life." It is a commitment that is both final and progressive as it enlarges in applications and details.

There is danger in assuming that consecration means the end of personal responsibility—that it takes away the need for courage, disciplined intelligence, and old-fashioned gumption. God does not work independently of but in and through the abilities, talents, and gifts He gives. Our lives are the gift of God to us; what we make of them is our gift to God. As John Seamands notes, "At the moment [of initial consecration] we can only affirm our willingness to decide in God's favor whenever we become aware of some specific issue before us."[8]

It is reported that on August 23, 1864, Abraham Lincoln wrote a resolution on a piece of paper, folded it, and asked his cabinet to endorse it with their signatures without reading it. They did so, committing themselves to whatever the president had resolved. So we put our signatures to the will of God although its details are yet unknown to us—in confidence that our Heavenly Father is too wise to make a mistake and too good to be unkind.

The Privilege Side of Consecration

Consecration under the Lordship of Jesus is an imperative of obedient love; but it is also an inestimable privilege with benefits beyond anything we can imagine. Christ asks of us everything we have in order to give us everything we need. As Hannah Whitall Smith said, If you go in on what she called "the privilege side of consecration . . . from the universal testimony of all who have tried it, . . . you will find it the happiest place you ever entered yet."[9]

For one thing, the Lordship of Jesus saves us from the scattering of interests and efforts that is the bane of so many Christian lives. Instead of Paul's "This one thing I do" (Phil. 3:13, KJV), it is "These many things I dabble in." A student in a campus prayer meeting testified how blessed he had been since he had "concentrated" his "life to the Lord." Concentration is the essence of consecration.

Paul Tournier, the Swiss evangelical physician-psychiatrist, spoke of the surrender he made to God after he had been a Christian for some time. It was not, he said, a limiting thing. It did not mean that he gave up the normal activities of his life. "What I was giving up," he said, "was my claim to act in accordance with my own will, in order to allow myself to be led as much as possible by God."

The result, Tournier continued, was "considerable relaxation of tension, especially in the case of anyone as anxious by nature as I am."

Nor was this a temporary matter. "This relaxation is greater still when God, through old age, relieves me of various responsibilities which he had laid upon me. It is also the answer to the problem of the 'unfulfilled.' . . . We can surrender to God all the worry about the things we have left uncompleted."[10]

Methodist missionary-evangelist E. Stanley Jones linked

consecration under the Lordship of Jesus with true spiritual maturity. He saw the great principle of life to be losing one's life to find it again. This occurs in three stages: "Dependence—the childhood stage; independence—the adolescent stage; interdependence—the mature stage."

It is in the stage of interdependence, Dr. Jones went on, that "we sovereignly take our independence and surrender it to a higher entity, the individual to the home, the citizen to the state, nation, world, the Christian to the kingdom of God." In each case, the surrender of sovereignty leads to a higher fellowship. To the degree that we discover this, we become mature. To the degree that we refuse to surrender to the higher relationship, we remain immature. "We become mature persons by self-surrender. So self-surrender is written, not merely in the Bible. It is written into the very nature of our relationships and hence inescapable."[11]

We noted earlier the consecration hymn written by Frances Ridley Havergal. Miss Havergal wrote her personal testimony in one of her books:

> It was Advent Sunday, December, 1873, that I first saw clearly the blessedness of true consecration. I saw it as a flash of electric light; and what you see, you cannot unsee. There must be full surrender before there can be true blessedness. God admits you by the one into the other. He Himself showed me this. First, I was shown the blood of Jesus Christ, His Son, cleanseth from all sin; and then it was made plain to me that He Who had cleansed me, had power to keep clean; so I utterly yielded myself to Him, and utterly trusted Him to keep me.

The key to it all is the statement, "There must be full surrender before there can be true blessedness." When we give ourselves to God, we become His property, and He is pledged to protect and care for what belongs to Him. "I know whom I have believed, and am convinced that he is able to guard what I have entrusted to him for that day" (2 Tim. 1:12).

One of Dwight Moody's favorite sayings was, "Give your

life to God. He can do more with it than you can." When a young medical student came to Mr. Moody in London for counsel, the evangelist said to him, "Young man, let God have your life. He can do more with it than you can." That was the turning point for young Grenfell—later Sir Wilfred Grenfell, the noted missionary doctor whose life and service were a blessing to multitudes.

George Macdonald, the Scottish minister-author, wrote lines he simply titled "Obedience":

I said, "Let me walk in the fields."
He said, "No, walk in the town."
I said, "There are no flowers there."
He said, "No flowers, but a crown."

I said, "But the skies are black;
There is nothing but noise and din."
He wept as He sent me back;
"There is more," He said, "there is sin."

I said, "I shall miss the light,
And friends will miss me, they say."
He answered, "Choose tonight
If I am to miss you, or they."

I pleaded for time to be given.
He said, "Is it hard to decide?
It will not seem hard in heaven
To have followed the steps of your Guide."

I cast one look at the field,
Then set my face to the town;
He said, "My child, do you yield?
Will you leave the flowers for the crown?"

Then into His hand went mine,
And into my heart came He;
And I walk in a light divine
The path I had feared to see.

4

CLEANSING: INTERNALIZING THE LORDSHIP OF JESUS

The temple of the Lord must be clean. It is sacrilege to ask the holy Christ to dwell in uncleansed temples. Jesus must be Lord not only of our outer lives; He must be Lord of our inner being, the very depths of our selves. This points to purity, the internalizing of His Lordship.

Most of us remember John Wesley's familiar distinction between justification and sanctification in the Christian life. Justification, he said, is Christ *for* us with the Father. Sanctification, on the other hand, is Christ *in* us by His Spirit. Justification is what happens objectively for us in the mind of God. Sanctification is what happens subjectively in us by the indwelling Spirit with whom we receive the Father and the Son (John 14:15-17, 23).

The Cleansing Baptism

The ministry of Jesus the Lord was introduced by John the Baptist. John presented himself as a forerunner. The importance of what he preached and did was to be known in the One who was to come after him. John's famous dictum, repeated in one way or another in all four Gospels, was that Jesus is the One who baptizes His people with the Holy Spirit.

"I baptize you with water for repentance," John said. "But after me will come one who is more powerful than I, whose sandals I am not fit to carry. He will baptize you with the Holy Spirit and with fire. His winnowing fork is in his hand, and he will clear his threshing floor, gathering his wheat into the barn and burning up the chaff with unquenchable fire" (Matt. 3:11-12; cf. Mark 1:8; Luke 3:16-17; John 1:33).

The clearing or cleansing of the threshing floor has sometimes been taken to refer to the final separation of righteous and wicked at the coming judgment of the Lord. But the word used is the Greek verb *diakatharizō,* to thoroughly cleanse or purify; and the root is frequently used throughout the New Testament to relate to the inner purifying of the human heart.

Fire is the symbol of purifying in Scripture, and the Holy Spirit "as fire" cleanses those whom Christ baptizes. When Peter described the results of Pentecost in the lives of the disciples in Acts 15:9, he said that the gift of the Spirit had the effect of "purifying *[katharisas]* their hearts by faith" (KJV).

J. Sidlow Baxter quotes Reuben A. Torrey, the Congregational evangelist who became the first president of the Moody Bible Institute and pastor of Moody Memorial Church in Chicago:

> There is nothing that cleanses like fire. If I have a piece of gold, and there is dirt on the outside, and I want to get the dirt off, I can take soap and water, perhaps, and wash it off. But suppose that the dirt is in the very metal itself, there is only one way to get it out—throw it into the fire! Just so with you and me. . . . The fire of the Holy Spirit consumes those things within us which are displeasing to God . . . uncleanness of all kinds.

Baxter adds, "I too believe in the refining fire of the Holy Spirit. With every fibre of conviction, I believe that the New Testament opens to us an inward purifying and refining of our whole moral nature. I believe that Charles Wesley's famous stanza not only expresses the deepest longing of all Christian hearts, but exactly echoes the accents of the New Testament itself—

Refining Fire, go through my heart,
Illuminate my soul;
Scatter Thy life through every part,
And sanctify the whole."[1]

This matter of purity is the crucial difference between those who understand the New Testament teaching about the sanctified life in the mode of John Wesley and his followers, and those who understand it in terms of empowerment without purity of heart. The distinctive mark of the Wesleyan position is its claim to a real cleansing of the moral nature by the indwelling Christ in the Spirit's fullness.

Daniel Steele, the Methodist theologian-educator of the last generation, calls attention to the fact that the Greek language abounds in words meaning repression or suppression. As many as 10 of these occur in the New Testament. They are translated variously: to bind, bruise, cast down, bring into bondage, repress, hinder, restrain, subdue, take by the throat. Yet none of these is ever used of inbred sin or sin in the heart. Rather such verbs are used as signify to cleanse, to purify, to mortify or kill, to crucify, and to destroy. Steele says:

> We have diligently sought in both the Old Testament and the New, for exhortations to seek the repression of sin. The uniform command is to put away sin, to purify the heart, to purge out the old leaven, to seek to be sanctified throughout spirit, soul, and body. Repressive power is nowhere ascribed to the blood of Christ, but rather purifying efficacy. Now if these verbs, which signify to cleanse, wash, crucify, mortify, or make dead, and to destroy, are all used in a metaphorical sense, it is evident that the literal truth signified is something far stronger than repression. It is eradication, extinction of being, destruction.[2]

There is, to be sure, a proper use of the terms repression, suppression, or counteraction. Howard V. Miller in his classic book *The Sin Problem* has two chapters, one on "Scriptural

Suppression" and the other on "Scriptural Counteraction." But Miller is entirely correct when he identifies the object of such suppression and counteraction as not the sinfulness of an unsanctified heart but the human drives, instincts, urges, and motivations that if not disciplined and controlled will defeat the plan of God for our lives.

The Pure in Heart

The Lord Jesus himself said in the Sermon on the Mount, "Blessed are the pure *[katharoi]* in heart, for they will see God" (Matt. 5:8). This is the internalizing of His Lordship, and the sphere is the heart.

Even a quick glance at a Bible concordance shows the importance the writers of Scripture place upon what they call the human "heart." The Old Testament uses words for "heart" more than 800 times, and the New Testament 164 times. While we tend to think of heart in terms of feeling, the Bible speaks of heart as the whole of the inner life. We love with our hearts (Mark 12:30), we purpose in our hearts (Dan. 1:8, KJV), and we think with our hearts (Matt. 9:4).

God's first call to us is, "Give me your heart" (Prov. 23:26). This is the first step into the Christian life—a call to trust, loyalty, and obedience. The result is the taking away of the "stony heart" of the unregenerated, and a "new heart" and a "new spirit" being placed within (Ezek. 36:26, KJV).

But the reach of redemption does not stop with the impartation of life to a dead soul. Over and over, God calls His people to that grace the Scripture calls "a pure heart" or "a clean heart." To "ascend the hill of the LORD" and to "stand in his holy place"—both in worship and in final destiny—demands "clean hands and a pure heart" (Ps. 24:3-4). With a spiritual instinct greater than the light available in his day, the Psalmist prayed, "Cleanse me with hyssop, and I will be clean . . . Create in me a pure heart, O God" (51:7, 10) and proclaimed God's special goodness "to those who are pure in heart" (73:1).

In the New Testament, Paul sees the goal of all God's commandments to be "love, which comes from a pure heart and a good conscience and a sincere faith" (1 Tim. 1:5). He urges his young friend and helper to "flee the evil desires of youth, and pursue righteousness, faith, love and peace, along with those who call on the Lord out of a pure heart" (2 Tim. 2:22).

James echoes the words of Ps. 24:4 in the context of Christian experience and life when he says, "Wash your hands, you sinners, and purify your hearts, you double-minded" (James 4:8).

Peter, who had commented that the most memorable result of Pentecost was "purifying their hearts by faith" (Acts 15:9, KJV), later wrote, "Seeing ye have purified your souls in obeying the truth through the Spirit unto unfeigned love of the brethren, see that ye love one another with a pure heart fervently" (1 Pet. 1:22, KJV).

The evidence is even more extensive than can be given here. The question is, What does it mean to have a pure heart?

This question has an urgency for us it did not necessarily have for our fathers. We live in a post-Freudian, psychologically oriented age. We have been told about the subconscious depths of personality in which are said to lurk motives and maladjustments of which we are never fully aware. We are warned, in view of this, not to witness to a cleansing of which we cannot be sure.

How Can We Know?

The warning has a validity we should not ignore. But we need to remember three facts in relation to what the Bible says about inner cleansing and the grace of a pure heart.

1. The Bible is not talking about a purity that would possibly satisfy the definitions of a depth psychologist. It is talking about a purity that satisfies the requirement of a holy God.

When we talk about the grace of a pure heart, we do not necessarily mean what Sigmund Freud would have meant had he ever imagined such a possibility. We are talking about what the Word of God means by a pure heart.

2. The promises of Scripture do not depend for their validation on our powers of introspection. We cannot affirm that our hearts are pure in a biblical sense because we do not detect defilement within.

But the situation here is no different than it is in regard to the forgiveness of sins. We do not believe our sins are forgiven because we are able to scan the record in God's book of life and see that the page is clear. We believe our sins are forgiven because the Bible declares, "If we confess our sins, he is faithful and just and will forgive us our sins and purify us from all unrighteousness" (1 John 1:9). In this faith, "The Spirit himself testifies with our spirit that we are God's children" (Rom. 8:16).

In a similar way, we believe sanctified hearts are pure because the Word declares, "But if we walk in the light as He is in the light, we have fellowship with one another, and the blood of Jesus Christ His Son cleanses us from all sin" (1 John 1:7, NKJV). Any who deny the need for such cleansing, John says, are self-deceived and the truth is not in them (v. 8). And here, as in the witness of the Spirit to the new birth, multitudes of God's people have found that they "have not received the spirit of the world but the Spirit who is from God, that we may understand what God has freely given us" (1 Cor. 2:12).

3. Both in Scripture and in experience it is clear that a pure heart does not mean that all emotional tangles are sorted out, all maladjustments are corrected, or the need for discipline and growth ended. A pure heart may be immature, at times troubled, sorely tempted, tried as by fire. A pure heart does not necesarily mean a clear mind. We can walk in fellowship with God with wrong ideas in our heads, but not with wrong attitudes in our hearts.

Negatively, a pure heart is one in which the inwardness of sin has been decisively dealt with by the grace of God. The deep-seated aversion of an unsanctified heart to the will of God has been corrected. Sören Kierkegaard was very close to the full truth when he wrote, "Purity of heart is to will one thing." That one thing is the will of God.

Sin as a condition of the heart is basically being out of tune with God. In Morton Dorsey's unforgettable metaphor, when a violinist tunes the string to perfect pitch we do not wonder where the "out-of-tuneness" went. If the string later gets out of tune, we do not wonder how the "out-of-tuneness" got back into the string.

Albert Edward Day writes, "To be pure . . . means getting rid of everything that is unjust, contentious, wrathful, uncharitable, resentful, fearful, snobbish, 'high hat,' opinionated, prejudiced, arrogant, sluggish, short-sighted, sectional, sectarian, racial (in the narrow sense), fanatical, unreal."[3]

Positively and more importantly, a pure heart is a heart bathed in and filled with the love of God "poured out . . . into our hearts by the Holy Spirit, whom he has given us" (Rom. 5:5). Never in a thousand years could we beat the darkness out of the cellar with a club. The way to get the darkness out is to let in the light. As Meister Eckhart, the 13th-century German mystic, put it, "A pure heart is one that . . . does not want its own way about everything, but which, rather is submerged in the loving will of God."[4]

One weakness in traditional ways of presenting the holiness message is that it has too often stopped with the negative death to self and freedom from sin. These are real and precious. But there's more to holiness than the absence of sin, just as there's more to light than the absence of darkness.

A pure heart is one conditioned by the indwelling Spirit of Christ to love God with all the heart, soul, mind, and strength, and one's neighbor as himself. Holiness is Christ reigning within, His love and His Spirit in control.

Holiness by faith in Jesus,
Not by efforts of your own;
Sin's dominion crushed and broken
By the power of grace alone:

God's own holiness within thee,
His own beauty on thy brow,
This shall be thy pilgrim brightness,
This thy blessed portion now.

—Frances Ridley Havergal

The Lord's Great Promise

In what has come to be called the Last Supper Discourse, the Lord Jesus gave His greatest promise to the disciples He was about to leave. It concerned the coming of the Holy Spirit, who, in the plan of God, was to accomplish for Christ's disciples the grace of a pure heart. It was a promise made under the shadow of the Cross.

The full scope of the promise was given in what scholars call The Paraclete Sayings (John 14:15-18, 25-27; 15:26-27; 16:5-15), so called from the Greek title for the Spirit used by Jesus, the *Paraklētos,* the Comforter, Counselor, Advocate, Helper. It is summarized in the first of these sayings: "If you love me, you will obey what I command. And I will ask the Father, and he will give you another Counselor to be with you forever—the Spirit of truth. The world cannot accept him, because it neither sees him nor knows him. But you know him, for he lives with you and will be in you. . . . If anyone loves me, he will obey my teaching. My Father will love him, and we will come to him and make our home with him" (John 14:15-17, 23).

This is a gift promised to those who love and obey the Lord Christ, a gift not available to the world. He comes, Jesus says, not as a stranger. The disciples know the Comforter, already experienced in the sense of forgiveness and the power of a new birth. And He comes, not as we have sometimes supposed, to replace Jesus but rather to make Him real—as we see in the rephrasing of the promise in verse 23: "My Father will love him, and we will come to him and make our home with him."

It is important to notice that the terms "in" and "with" are not used in a spatial sense, since the Holy Spirit "in" the believer is the equivalent of the Father and Son "with" the believer. These are relational terms. Just as an acquaintance may become a very dear friend, a doctor who has been a physician may serve as a surgeon when the need arises, and a fiancé may become a bridegroom, so the Holy Spirit who has been the regenerating life is to become the sanctifying Lord, enthroning the Triune Deity within in what Paul called "all the fullness of God" (Eph. 3:19). As Christopher Wordsworth wrote:

He has raised our human nature
In the clouds to God's right hand;
There we sit in heavenly places,
There with Him in glory stand:
Jesus reigns, adored by angels;
Man with God is on the throne;
Mighty Lord, in Thine ascension
We by faith behold our own.

Glory be to God the Father,
Glory be to God the Son,
Dying, risen, ascending for us,
Who the heavenly realm has won;
Glory to the Holy Spirit,
To one God in Persons Three,
Glory both in earth and heaven,
Glory, endless glory be!

The Cost of the Internalized Lordship

All this comes to us through the obedience of the Servant Lord. He was given the name above all names by reason of the fact that He "humbled himself and became obedient to death—even death on a cross!" (Phil. 2:8). The sacrifice of Christ makes possible for us the Father's full forgiveness. The Cross also makes possible our cleansing.

The giving love of God the Father is expressed in the Golden Text of the Bible: "For God so loved the world that he gave his one and only Son, that whoever believes in him shall not perish but have eternal life" (John 3:16). But the great parallel is Eph. 5:25-27, "Christ loved the church and gave himself up for her to make her holy, cleansing her by the washing with water through the word, and to present her to himself as a radiant church, without stain or wrinkle or any other blemish, but holy and blameless."

The writer to the Hebrews three times refers to this fact. "By that will [of God as wrought in Jesus at Calvary], we have been made holy through the sacrifice of the body of Jesus Christ once for all" (10:10). "By one sacrifice he has made perfect forever those who are being made holy" (v. 14). "And so Jesus also suffered outside the city gate to make the people holy through his own blood" (13:12).

One of the most familiar and precious promises is inscribed in 1 John 1:7. "But if we walk in the light, as he is in the light, we have fellowship with one another, and the blood of Jesus, his Son, purifies us from all sin." The outstanding British New Testament scholar B. F. Westcott comments: "The Blood brings about that real sinlessness which is essential to union with God. . . . The sin is done away; and the purifying action is exerted continuously. . . . The thought here is of 'sin' and not of 'sins,' of the spring, the principle, and not of the separate manifestations."[5]

Farewell! Henceforth my place
Is with the Lamb Who died:
My Sovereign, while I have Thy love,
What could I want beside?

Thyself, dear Lord, art now
My free and loving choice,
"In Whom, though now I see Thee not,
Believing, I rejoice."

Shame on me that I sought
Another joy than this,
Or dreamt a heart at rest with Thee
Could crave for earthly bliss.
These vain and worthless things,
I put them all aside:
His goodness fills my longing soul,
And I am satisfied.[6]

5

THE CONTINUING LORDSHIP OF JESUS

The Lordship of Jesus is established in our lives in those great moments of grace we call conversion and entire sanctification. But the purpose of the moments goes beyond them to an ongoing life. Paul's prayer for the young Christians at Thessalonica indicates this: "May God himself, the God of peace, sanctify you through and through. May your whole spirit, soul and body be kept blameless at [or until] the coming of our Lord Jesus Christ" (1 Thess. 5:23).

What begins with Christ's enthronement as Lord of all the kingdoms of the soul is an ongoing, progressive life. Jesus himself is the personal embodiment of this life-ideal. "We [are] in all things [to] grow up into him who is the Head, that is, Christ" (Eph. 4:15). "We, who with unveiled faces all reflect the Lord's glory, are being transformed into his likeness with ever-increasing glory, which comes from the Lord, who is the Spirit" (2 Cor. 3:18).

Over and over, the New Testament indicates this. It is God's eternal purpose: "For those God foreknew he also predestined to be conformed to the likeness of his Son, that he might be the firstborn among many brothers" (Rom. 8:29). As John put it, "Dear friends, now we are children of God, and what we will be has not yet been made known. But we know that when he appears, we shall be like him, for we shall see him as he is. Everyone who has this hope in him purifies himself, just as he is pure" (1 John 3:2-3).

To be more like the Lord Jesus is the end for which the epochs of grace are the means. To know more and more of His love and compassion, His gentleness and forgiveness, His humility, courage, humor, His totally selfless humanness—this is the lifelong meaning of the Lordship of Jesus for each of us.

The Mind of Christ

One aspect of this ongoing life is suggested in the great Christological passage in Philippians 2 to which we have before referred. Paul's interest is immediately practical. He writes about the self-emptying of Christ, His humility, His obedience even unto death in order to reinforce the injunction of verse 5, "Let this mind be in you which was also in Christ Jesus" (NKJV). "We have the mind of Christ" (1 Cor. 2:16).

Certainly, there is much about the mind of Christ we can never comprehend. To fully know another mind would require a mind equal to the one known. Only a mathematician of equal stature could fully understand the equations of an Albert Einstein.

The Bible clearly teaches that there are aspects of the divine mind we shall never grasp.

> "For my thoughts are not your thoughts,
> neither are your ways my ways," declares the LORD.
> "As the heavens are higher than the earth,
> so are my ways higher than your ways
> and my thoughts than your thoughts" *(Isa. 55:8-9).*

Paul closes the profound theological section of his letter to the Romans with a hymn to the all-surpassing wisdom of God:

> Oh, the depth of the riches of the wisdom and knowledge of God!
> How unsearchable his judgments, and his paths beyond tracing out!

"Who has known the mind of the Lord?
Or who has been his counselor?" *(Rom. 11:33-34).*

In a sense, then, we are always seeking the mind of Christ. Our Lord's will is known in clear and broad outlines, but we may not always be certain of the details. In fact, there is reason to be suspicious of those who with complete dogmatism assert, "The Lord told me . . ." and "God said . . . ," especially when the content of those statements is other than a direct quotation from the Bible in context.

This does not mean that God does not reveal His will in specific instances to open and obedient minds. But He normally does it through a combination of indicators.

There is a well-known incident told by F. B. Meyer that gives the clue. Meyer was on a little coastal steamer sailing across the Irish Sea from England. The night was overcast, without light of moon or stars. The channel into the Irish harbor was difficult to navigate, yet the vessel was approaching the entrance at full steam.

Meyer stood by the helmsman and asked, "Man, how do you ever find your way into the harbor on a night like this?"

"It's no problem," replied the sailor. "You see those three lights in line on the hillside ahead? Those lights are our beacon. When they are lined up in a straight line, we know we are right on course down the middle of the channel."

Meyer repeatedly used this as an illustration of the way God guides in specific choices. The lights are the Word of God, the open door of circumstances under His sovereign control, and the inner impression in the soul. When all three are "in line," we may go ahead with confidence.

Christ's Mind in Us

Yet in another sense there is a "givenness" about the mind of Christ. "We have the mind of Christ." "Let this mind be in you which was also in Christ Jesus."

One of John Wesley's favorite descriptions of the sanctified state was "the mind which was in Christ." This, he said, he saw "in a clearer and clearer light" from the beginning of his spiritual pilgrimage to be an "indispensable necessity."[1] When we have "a pure intention of heart," then "is that mind in us, which was also in Christ Jesus."[2]

Wesley defined one who is "perfect" as "one in which is 'the mind which was in Christ,' and who so 'walketh as Christ also walked'; a man 'that hath clean hands and a pure heart,' or that is 'cleansed from all filthiness of the flesh and spirit'; one in whom there is 'no occasion of stumbling,' and who, accordingly, 'does not commit sin.'"[3]

We may understand this better when we note that the word Paul used in Phil. 2:5 is not the broader New Testament word for mental activities or the content of thought *(nous).* It is *phronēma,* a term that carries the thought of mind-set or disposition—less adequately, "attitude" as in the NIV. It is the same term used when Paul contrasts the mind of the flesh with the mind of the Spirit in Rom. 8:5-7. We cannot know all Christ knows, but we can share His mind-set, His disposition or attitude.

What is this mind-set or disposition? A brief answer is given in the verses that follow Phil. 2:5—humility; freedom from selfish ambition and vain conceit, or ambition for position and following; self-giving; and obedience at whatever cost. The one time Jesus described His own character, He said, "I am gentle and humble in heart" (Matt. 11:28-30).

An expanded description is given in Gal. 5:22-23, Paul's listing of the fruit of the Spirit which Friedrich Schleiermacher called "the virtues of Christ"—a portrait of the disposition and character of Jesus. The ninefold list is well known: loving, joyous, serene, patient, kind, good, faithful, gentle, and self-controlled.

Later in Philippians (4:8) in more general terms, Paul describes the ideal Christian mind. It is occupied with what is true, noble, right, pure, lovely, admirable, excellent, and praiseworthy.

The true is the real, genuine, enduring as opposed to the deceptive and illusory. The noble, William Barclay says, "has the dignity of holiness about it" as contrasted with the flippant, cheap, and tawdry.

The right is what is due and proper against that which appeals to self-interest alone. The pure is the morally undefiled; that which is not sordid or shabby, soiled or smutty.

The lovely is the attractive, the winsome, expressing itself in kindness, sympathy, and forbearance. The admirable is the gracious (the Greek word is associated with worship)—"fit for God to hear."

The excellent is that of superior worth, and the praiseworthy is that approved by good men and above all in the sight of God.[4]

The apostle himself is a role model for this kind of thinking: "Whatever you have learned or received or heard from me, or seen in me—put it into practice" (v. 9).

Paul's description of truly Christian thinking is framed with two remarkable promises. Before are the words, "And the peace of God, which transcends all understanding, will guard your hearts and your minds in Christ Jesus" (v. 7). After is the assurance, "And the God of peace will be with you" (v. 9).

The Centrality of Love

At the heart of it all is divine love as the ruling attitude of the mind that was in Christ Jesus. Late in the ministry of the Master, a noteworthy encounter took place. A Pharisee identified as a teacher of the law challenged Jesus with the question, "Of all the commandments, which is the most important?" When one remembers that the scribes had identified 613 "commandments" in the law and tradition, this was a good question.

In answer, Jesus turned to the Old Testament. He put together a statement from the famous Shema of Deuteronomy 6, and one from the Holiness Code in Leviticus 19, and said, "The most important one is this: 'Hear, O Israel, the Lord our God, the Lord is one. Love the Lord your God with all your heart and with all your soul and with all your mind and with all your strength.' The second is this: 'Love your neighbor as yourself.' There is no commandment greater than these."

The reply of the interrogator was, "Well said, teacher. You are right in saying that God is one and there is no other but him. To love him with all your heart, with all your understanding, and with all your strength, and to love your neighbor as yourself is more important than all burnt offerings and sacrifices."

And Mark comments, "When Jesus saw that he had answered wisely, he said to him, 'You are not far from the kingdom of God'" (Mark 12:28-34). We may only speculate whether the scribe made it into the Kingdom. But one point is clear: God's kingdom is a kingdom whose law is love.

Over and over the New Testament points to this. God himself *is* love (1 John 4:8, 16). The new commandment of Jesus to His disciples was "Love one another; as I have loved you" (John 13:34, KJV). "Love is the fulfilling of the law" (Rom. 13:10, KJV). The highest in Christian experience is described as being "made perfect in love" (1 John 4:18).

John Wesley described "the pure in heart" as one in whom "love has purified his heart from envy, malice, wrath, and every unkind temper."[5] In answer to the question, "What is Christian perfection?" Wesley replied, "The loving God with all our heart, mind, soul, and strength. This implies, that no wrong temper, none contrary to love, remains in the soul."[6]

In an age when many are preoccupied with gifts and miracles, we need to hear Wesley's words:

> Love is the highest gift of God; humble, gentle, patient love; that all visions, revelations, manifestations whatever, are little

things compared to love. . . . The heaven of heavens is love. There is nothing higher in religion; there is, in effect, nothing else; if you look for anything but more love, you are looking wide of the mark, you are getting out of the royal way. And when you are asking others, "Have you received this or that blessing?" if you mean anything but more love, you mean wrong; you are leading them out of the way, and putting them upon a false scent. Settle it then in your heart, that from the moment God has saved you from all sin, you are to aim at nothing more, but more of that love described in the thirteenth chapter of [First] Corinthians. You can go no higher than this, till you are carried into Abraham's bosom.[7]

When asked about the properties or fruits of such love, Wesley did as he suggested. He turned to 1 Cor. 13:4-7—words well worth pondering in an age that thinks of love as anything from Hollywood to heaven and that uses the term "luv" to describe everything from a small pickup truck to disposable diapers: "Love is patient, love is kind. It does not envy, it does not boast, it is not proud. It is not rude, it is not self-seeking, it is not easily angered, it keeps no record of wrongs. Love does not delight in evil but rejoices with the truth. It always protects, always trusts, always hopes, always perseveres."[8]

Lord of the Future

To His called-out and gathered Church, Jesus gave His great promise and commission: "All authority in heaven and on earth has been given to me. Therefore go and make disciples of all nations, baptizing them in the name of the Father and of the Son and of the Holy Spirit, and teaching them to obey [all] I have commanded you. And surely I am with you always, to the very end of the age" (Matt. 28:18-20). Here are four inclusive "alls": *all* authority or power; to *all* nations; teaching *all* that is commanded; with His presence always, for *all* time.

Jesus *is* Lord. This is a fact demonstrated in His resurrection and ascension. It is a fact cherished by millions throughout the ages, but unknown to even more millions. "For this very reason, Christ died and returned to life so that he might be the Lord of both the dead and the living" (Rom. 14:9). He has been given "the name . . . above every name, that at the name of Jesus every knee should bow, in heaven and on earth and under the earth, and every tongue confess that Jesus Christ is Lord, to the glory of God the Father" (Phil. 2:9-11).

In His nature, what Christ was with the Father through the ages, He was in His life on earth—with one exception: "He emptied himself," as Charles Wesley sang, "of all but love," of every attribute of Deity that would prevent Him from entering our human experience to the full. He is now glorified again with the glory He had with the Father from all eternity (John 17:5).

Known to All as King

But the gospel is incomplete without the awareness that "this same Jesus . . . will come back in the same way" He ascended into heaven (Acts 1:11). He will come again, not to be despised and rejected by men, but to reign as King of Kings and Lord of Lords.

Jesus came the first time incognito, recognized by only a minority; He comes again unveiled in the full truth of His nature. He came the first time in humanity; He comes again in the glory of His full deity, His oneness with the Father. He came the first time in weakness; He comes again in power. He came the first time to save; He comes again to judge.

We know not *when* Christ will come again; we are sure *that* He is coming. Jesus himself gave only one precise historical sign of His approaching return. Jerusalem would be trodden down by the Gentiles until the times of the Gentiles are fulfilled (Luke 21:24). In May 1948, the 1,900-year Gentile domination of Jerusalem was brought to an abrupt end. There is now no identifiable historical condition that must occur before Jesus the Lord comes again. While we plan our lives as if we would live out the normal span of life on this earth, we must live our lives in daily readiness for the King's coming.

The Completed Lordship

This is the completed Lordship of Jesus—to be known and acknowledged by every conscious being in the universe: angels in heaven, people on earth, the powers of darkness "under the earth" (Phil. 2:10). Christ reigning inwardly now as Savior and Lord is our "hope of glory" (Col. 1:27). Then His Lordship will come to full fruition for us.

The Kingdom of grace will become the Kingdom of glory. "Our citizenship is in heaven. And we eagerly await a Savior from there, the Lord Jesus Christ, who, by the power that enables him to bring everything under his control, will transform our lowly bodies so that they will be like his glorious body" (Phil. 3:20-21).

The hosts of evil may seem to gain the upper hand. Demonic powers seek to rule the world. But they are subject to the final purpose of Christ. The kingdoms of the world must become what they are in fact—the kingdoms of our Lord and of His Christ. The scenario of the Book of Revelation will be played out to the full.

A Roman emperor known as Julian the Apostate was a tragic interlude in the history of the Early Church. He was a nephew of Constantine the Great—the Constantine who had removed all the restrictions against Christianity that had existed for the preceding two centuries. Julian had been raised in a Christian environment but had turned away and had gone back to paganism.

When Julian became emperor at age 29, he determined to bring back the old gods and destroy the Christian Church. In the 18 months of his reign, bitter persecution against the Christians broke out.

During this interlude, a pagan Roman said with a sneer to

his Christian neighbor, "And where is your Galilean carpenter now?"

The simple reply was, "He is building a coffin for your emperor."

The oldest histories of the Christian Church record that just a few months later, in a battle in Persia, Julian received a mortal wound. It is said that he took a handful of his own life's blood, flung it into the air in a gesture of defeat, and cried, "You have conquered, O Galilean!"

Conquer indeed He shall. This is our confidence. Our place is to give ourselves completely to His authority. He must be to us not only Savior but Lord. When His will is done in us, we shall be ready for the time when His will is done on earth as it is now done in heaven. Then it will be worth it all to have lived under the Lordship of Jesus in the purity and power of His Spirit.

There is a faith unmixed with doubt,
A love all free from fear;
A walk with Jesus, where is felt
His presence always near.
There is a rest that God bestows
Transcending pardon's peace,
A lowly, sweet simplicity,
Where inward conflicts cease.

There is a service God-inspired,
A zeal that timeless grows,
Where self is crucified with Christ,
And joy unceasing flows.
There is a being "right with God"
That yields to His commands
Unswerving, true fidelity,
A loyalty that stands.

There is a purity of heart,
A cleanness of desire,

Wrought by the Holy Comforter
With sanctifying fire.
There is a glory that awaits
Each Blood-washed soul on high,
When Christ returns to take His Bride
With Him beyond the sky.

—KENNETH WELLS

Notes

Chapter 1. JESUS IS LORD

1. Werner Foerster, "*Kurios,* etc." in Gerhard Kittel, ed., *Theological Dictionary of the New Testament;* Geoffrey W. Bromiley, translator and editor (Grand Rapids: William B. Eerdmans Publishing Co., 1965), 3:1040.

2. An interesting sidelight concerns the decision of the Old Testament translators of the *American Standard Version,* published in 1901, to use the term "Jehovah" for *Yahweh.* "Jehovah" is a name made by taking the consonants of *Yahweh* and adding the vowels of *Adonai.* It was first used in the 16th century and is not a scriptural name at all. Originating about the same time that the ASV was becoming better known, the "Witnesses" chose it for the name of their religion.

3. Cf. also Ps. 102:25-27 as used in Heb. 1:10-12.

4. Cf. Rev. 1:8 where the terms Alpha and Omega are used of God.

Chapter 2. RECONCILIATION:
ACCEPTANCE OF THE LORDSHIP OF JESUS

1. John Macquarrie, *God and Secularity, New Directions in Theology Today* (Philadelphia: Westminster Press, 1967), 3:126.

2. Georgia Harkness, *Does God Care?* (Waco, Tex.: Word Books, 1960), 104.

3. A. W. Tozer, *The Knowledge of the Holy: The Attributes of God: Their Meaning in the Christian Life* (New York: Harper and Brothers, 1961), 117-18.

4. Alan Richardson, *An Introduction to the Theology of the New Testament* (New York: Harper and Brothers, 1958), 84-87.

5. John Wesley, *The Works of John Wesley,* reprint of the third edition (Kansas City: Beacon Hill Press of Kansas City, 1978), 6:509. Cf. Paul M. Bassett and William M. Greathouse, *Exploring Christian Holiness* (Kansas City: Beacon Hill Press of Kansas City, 1985), 2:209.

6. Henryk Sienkiewicz, *Quo Vadis?* trans. Jeremiah Curtain (Boston: Little, Brown, and Co., 1897), 167.

7. Cf. Paul S. Rees, *Triumphant in Trouble* (Westwood, N.J.: Fleming H. Revell Co., 1962), 37-38.

8. David A. Hubbard, *What's New?* (Waco, Tex.: Word Books, 1970), 37-38.

9. Billy Graham, *Approaching Hoofbeats: The Four Horsemen of the Apocalypse* (Minneapolis: Grason, 1983), 235-36.

Chapter 3. CONSECRATION:
ESTABLISHMENT OF THE LORDSHIP OF JESUS

1. In T. K. Thompson, ed., *Stewardship Facts, 1965-1966* (New York: Department of Publication Services, NCCCUSA, 1965), 65-66.

2. Thomas R. Kelly, *A Testament of Devotion* (New York: Harper and Row, Publishers, 1941), 49.

3. Frances Ridley Havergal, *Kept for the Master's Use* (New Canaan, Conn.: Keats Publishing, 1973 reprint), 89.

4. D. Shelby Corlett, *Lord of All* (Kansas City: Beacon Hill Press, 1962), 56.

5. Helen W. Kooiman, *Cameos: Women Fashioned by God* (Wheaton, Ill.: Tyndale House Publishers, 1968), 80.

6. Gerald Cragg, "Romans" (Exposition), *The Interpreter's Bible,* ed. George Buttrick (New York: Abingdon Press, 1952), 9:581.

7. Quoted by A. M. Hills, *Holiness in the Book of Romans* (Kansas City: Beacon Hill Press, 1950), 40.

8. John T. Seamands, *On Tiptoe with Love* (Kansas City: Beacon Hill Press of Kansas City, 1971), 87.

9. Hannah Whitall Smith, *The Christian's Secret of a Happy Life* (Westwood, N.J.: Fleming H. Revell Co., 1952), 50.

10. Paul Tournier, *Learn to Grow Old* (New York: Harper and Row, Publishers, 1972), 214.

11. E. Stanley Jones, *Victory Through Surrender* (New York: Abingdon Press, 1966), 78.

Chapter 4. CLEANSING:
INTERNALIZING THE LORDSHIP OF JESUS

1. J. Sidlow Baxter, *A New Call to Holiness* (Grand Rapids: Zondervan Publishing House, 1973), 199-200.

2. Quoted by Thomas C. Cook, *New Testament Holiness* (London: Epworth Press, 1952), 31.

3. Albert Edward Day, *Discipline and Discovery* (Nashville: Parthenon Press, 1961), 109.

4. Quoted by Cecil G. Osborne, *The Art of Understanding Yourself* (Grand Rapids: Zondervan Books, 1967), 37.

5. B. F. Westcott, *The Epistles of St. John* (London: Macmillan and Co., 1883), 20-21.

6. Quoted in Frederick P. Wood, *The Question of Worldliness* (London: Marshall, Morgan, and Scott, 1955), 70.

Chapter 5. THE CONTINUING LORDSHIP OF JESUS

1. John Wesley, *A Plain Account of Christian Perfection* (Kansas City: Beacon Hill Press of Kansas City, 1966 reprint), 11.

2. Ibid., 13.

3. Ibid., 36; cf. also 37, 38, 117, 118, 119.

4. William Barclay, *The Letters to the Philippians, Colossians, and Thessalonians,* "The Daily Bible Study" (Edinburgh: St. Andrew Press, 1961), 97-100.

5. Wesley, *Plain Account,* 19.

6. Ibid., 51.

7. Ibid., 99.

8. Cf. ibid., 81.